Passionate Intensity

Passionate Intensity

Linda Stitt

Seraphim Editions

© 2003 Linda Stitt

All rights reserved. No part of this publication may be reproduced or transmitted in any any form or by any means – electronic or mechanical, including photocopying, recording or any information storage and retrieval system – without written permission from the Publisher, except by a reviewer who wishes to quote brief passages for inclusion in a review.

The publisher gradefully acknowledges the financial assistance of the Canada Council for the Arts.

Published in 2003 by
Seraphim Editions
970 Queen Street East, P.O. Box 98174
Toronto, Ontario Canada M4M 1J0
http://www.seraphimeditions.com

National Library of Canada Cataloguing in Publication

Stitt, Linda, 1932-
 Passionate intensity / Linda Stitt.

Poems.
ISBN 0-9689723-7-3

 I. Title.

PS8587.T58P37 2003   C811'.54   C2002-905719-1
PR9199.3.S798P37 2003

Editor: Allan Briesmaster
Design: Paula Stitt and Morley Chalmers
Front cover photo by Tien Tran
Back cover lotus photo by Julie Schaeffer
Author photo by Paula Stitt

Set in 11 point Hoeffler
Printed and bound in Canada

The best lack all conviction, while the worst
Are full of passionate intensity.
        – William Butler Yeats, "The Second Coming"

I had considered calling this book *Lacking All Conviction*, but that seemed a little too presumptuous.

Autumnal Equinox

- 11   Carpe Poem
- 12   Relocation
- 13   Tripping
- 14   Resident Neurosis
- 15   Dancing with the Dark
- 16   Kitchen
- 17   January 7th 2001
- 18   Last Spring
- 20   Singularity
- 21   Making Light of Myself
- 22   Bette's Land
- 23   Coming to Terms
- 24   Oh Happy Day

Winter Solstice

- 27   I Heard a Song
- 28   Abandonment
- 29   Gone and Lost
- 30   Dental Appointment
- 31   Concrete Galoshes
- 32   Endurance Test
- 33   Family, Gathering
- 34   Sidetracks
- 35   Sin in my Seventieth Year

Vernal Equinox

- 39 Court Etiquette
- 41 Geriatric Valentine
- 42 Better Late
- 44 Falling Flat
- 45 Footnote
- 46 Mirrors
- 47 Bottom Line
- 48 Etymology
- 49 Exploring an Alien Civilization
- 50 No Free Lunch
- 51 Enemies
- 52 Epiphany
- 54 More of the Same
- 56 Figment
- 58 Minding My Business

Summer Solstice

- 63 Take Your Medicine
- 64 Non-determined
- 65 Fancy This
- 67 Effortless Practice
- 68 A Joyful Noise
- 70 Karuna
- 71 Solstice
- 72 Ground of Being
- 73 Last Word

Autumnal Equinox

CARPE POEM

Poetry is an imperative.
Like a timely tourniquet
or a full bladder,
it requires immediate attention.
It cannot be deferred.

It must be deferred to,
welcomed and entertained
whenever it comes to call.

Poetry makes no appointments,
accepts no invitations,
shows up at its own convenience
and will not be kept waiting.

Poetry postponed
does not hang around.
It slips away
the instant it is put on hold
and will not be retrieved.

If poetry comes to visit,
abandon all engagements,
brew it a cup
of your finest concentration,
pick up your pen
and accept the gift
of expression.

RELOCATION

When the past became too painful
and the future grew too fearful,
to try to dwell in either
made me terrified and tearful.
So I left them
and I carried with me
nothing but the present.

It's inordinately pleasant.

TRIPPING

A moment's journey takes, for me
on most occasions, hours and hours,
for many times I'm bound to pause
to write a poem or gather flowers.
And I am easily enticed
and very frequently distracted
for travel's pleasures lie in how
the path and I have interacted.
And even though I'm often lost
and even if the poems fail
and though I never may arrive,
blossoms are strewn along my trail.

RESIDENT NEUROSIS

Somewhere,
in some secluded cubbyhole,
in the depths of my psyche,
bounce the echoes
of the fear of abandonment.

In a place
I rarely visit consciously,
the occasional glimmer of light
has whitewashed the walls
and mopped the floors,
but still there remain
the dust and dregs of secrets.
It is, however,
not as dark as it was
and it smells better.

My shadow has moved,
        probably not out,
        but over.
It is, no doubt,
boogieing in some other closet
or lurking in the basement
in voluptuous obscurity.

I am in no great rush to discover it.
It will merely change its name
and relocate
to another apartment
in the same complex.

DANCING WITH THE DARK
OR
PAS DE PROBLÈME
OR
WHEN WE WERE VERY JUNG

Learn how to dance with your shadow.
She may be a little bit weird
but be kind and polite,
lead her into the light.
She isn't as bad as you feared.

She's a creature of your own creation,
the bogey-man under your bed
with only the power you give her,
so give her a giggle instead.

Reality is what we make it;
we see as we've chosen to see,
so broaden your view
and you'll see she's just you
 – perhaps as you'd rather not be.

But try, nonetheless, to embrace her,
there's every conceivable chance
that love will transform and transmute her
and then she will teach you to dance.

KITCHEN

I like to sit in the kitchen,
it's such an honest place,
a person's herself in the kitchen,
not wearing her company face.
And talk's down to earth in the kitchen
and casual clothes are fine.
        The dining room's too formal,
        I'd rather eat than dine.
We squeezed round the kitchen table
when I was a kid on the farm
and shared the doings of our days
knee to knee and arm to arm.
And the kitchen meant warmth and family
and the kitchen was secure.
The world could be dark and scary
but the kitchen was safe and sure.
And when you had a secret
you had to tell before you burst
or needed a hug, or a kiss for a hurt,
you went to the kitchen first.

I grew away from the kitchen
but I love to sit and look
and remember the sounds and smells and tastes
of someone who loved to cook.

JANUARY 7th 2001

This is the brightest night
that we will know.
Come outside with me
and dance upon the silvered ground.
Let us join hands and circle
to celebrate
the sharing
of abundant moonlight.
There is enough to go round.

LAST SPRING

By the end of May
the crocuses have disappeared.
The scilla have withered
and the tulips have turned themselves
inside-out, in ecstasy.

Spring is rushing past.
The petals of the apple blossoms
are following their fragrance
along the wind
and the daffodils and jonquils
are already drooping,
        past their prime.
The magnolias and forsythia
have shed their elegance
and gone on to mundane matters.

But phalanxes of lily of the valley
are marshalling their perfumed power
and the bleeding hearts
are dripping beneficence.

The gardens are parading
their paeans to the season
and at each step,
each note in the vernal panegyric,
I want to say
        Stop.
        Wait.
        I have not experienced you fully.
        I may not see your like again.

But if I do not manage not to cling,
the peonies will not explode.
The iris will not yet unfurl their flags.
The lilacs will still clench their redolent buds
and the roses
        oh, the roses!
could not proffer their delight.
Frozen, present beauty
would lock the gate
against the garden's growing glory.

And so, I let them go,
        all of the grace of yesterday,
        all of the revelations of today,
so that tomorrow's promises will ripen,
        summer's fruits, autumn's bounty
and I will slip, satiated,
into winter's barren wonder.

SINGULARITY

I am shrinking,
    not becoming shy,
        like a shrinking violet,
            but becoming shorter,
            dwindling in stature.
I was never formidable
but now I border on petite,
heading toward insignificant.

I look up more often
and frequently stand on my toes.
I am not particularly concerned;
size is of no great importance to me
unless it affects the fit of my clothes.
I do not feel compelled to measure up.

But I speculate and extrapolate.

Will I diminish
into the desiccated dregs
of an abandoned vessel,
to ride like sibylline dust
on the winds of eternity?

Or will the good things increase
as the package gets smaller,
growing more dense
till I collapse on myself
like a spent star,
drawing creation into me,
spinning light and matter
on my event horizon,
confounding space and time,
    as well as friends and family,
becoming my own tunnel
to another universe?

MAKING LIGHT OF MYSELF

All formations are impermanent.

I am wearing down,
wearing out,
wearing away.

There is now
only the finest hesitation
between matter
and cessation,
      only the finest clinging
      to delusion
      of separation.

Caught in the unending swirl
of galaxies,
      never arriving
      where I thought I was going,
I release expectation
and the certainty of knowing
how things ought to be.

Seeking to flee
the heaviness of form,
I prepare to free
the indentured flesh
and transform
my sight of myself,
making light of myself.

BETTE'S LAND

I am not put on this earth
to do harm to anything,
So cool it, Missus Blackbird,
I'm not here to hassle
your home in the bulrushes.
I don't intend to disturb the daisies
or the dragonflies.
I bear no malice to the mosquitoes,
      although I do not seek their company.
I will not tread upon the jeweled toad
or misalign the desiccated pine cones,
      blossoming in cross section.
I will breathe no poison into the air,
      set no unwary foot upon a seedling,
      drop no anger or ill will
      into the universal water.

For this moment,
on this ground,
unwholesomeness leaves me
and I am born, reborn and born again.

I will try, once more,
to carry purity of heart
back to a city
which does not forgive innocence.

COMING TO TERMS

Time and chance
have worn me quite away,
yet I may serve
without despair or wrath.

Even a broken pot
can sometimes hold
sufficient rain
to make a sparrow's bath.

OH HAPPY DAY

One breath today
draws joy
into the marrow of my bones,
    the chambers of my heart.
        I breathe one mind,
        the luminous totality,
        the consciousness that permeates each part
        of indivisible creation.
Nothing exists
except the self
in protean reality,
immanent, ineffable,
infinite manifestation.
        In every moment
        I inhale the love
        all being breathes to me
        in purest exhalation.

I see flowers underneath my feet,
rainbows arching overtop the street
and haloes crowning everyone I meet.

Winter Solstice

I HEARD A SONG

I heard a song you used to sing
and felt the loss afresh,
        blood that created my blood,
        flesh that bore my flesh.

How can it be
that what was everything to me
is only dust and memory?
How do they carry on,
the host
who lose the one
who loved them most?

Surely I cannot be the only one
whose grief
is past all bearing
and belief.

Time and acceptance,
I am told,
will help the wound to heal,
and I accept, and wait,
but that does not allay
the pain I feel,
lying beneath,
ready to rise and overwhelm me when
I hear a song you will not sing again.

ABANDONMENT

I was not done
with being your child;
I was still learning to love.
And it's all very well to say
I hold you in my heart
and that you teach me still
by memory
and by the code that forms my flesh.
But there's an emptiness
too vast for my embrace.

Sometimes, I see your spectre on the street
or seated with a cup of tea at hand
and, staggering with loss,
I move to take you in my arms,
to fit my cheek
into the hollow of your neck
and place my bulk
between the world
and your fragility.
But I cannot make you mine.
I cannot follow you
or bring you back
or, for my sins,
bestow your essence on another.

I could not have kept you,
ought not to bear the guilt
that taints my aimless grief,
do not begrudge you your release.
I let you go
and let you go
and let you go.
On my deathbed
I shall forgive you.

GONE AND LOST

Where has it gone,
        that subtle consciousness
        which shaped you
        and then fled the form,
            leaving us perpetually bereft?
Who are you
since the one we loved has left?
What womb gave you refuge
after your forty days
of wandering?
Which, now, are your ways?

What birth have you come to?
In what realm may I find you?
Have you forsaken
this planet, galaxy and universe?
Where did you awaken?
Do you recall what you have left behind you?

Are you beyond my prayers?

I know I will not feel your touch again.
Your voice fades like an echo in my mind
and yet today, as in the distant then,
my thoughts embrace you,
        as they always will.

Wherever and whoever and however you may be,
do you love me still?

DENTAL APPOINTMENT

My body
does not forgive easily.
I can feel it
circling in on itself,
protecting me
against impending pain.

I reason with myself,
instilling logic
into the cowering corners
of my mind,
telling myself
to temper dread,
to hold no grudges,
to forget past hurts,
but every cell remembers
and resists.

I am rigid
within my armour,
I cannot bend
to take the hand
of conciliation.

It is hard to trust
when the flesh does not forgive.

CONCRETE GALOSHES

My reality
is anchored by objects,
here a house,
there a tree,
around me a collection of possessions
that define me
    as
        wearer of silk,
        brusher of teeth,
        drinker of filtered water ...
But, lately, things are vanishing,
    a hat
    a scarf,
    two umbrellas in one week,
    my mother's ring,
each taking with them
        a bit of my identity,
        a piece of my persona,
        a layer of the lacquer
        that holds my ego in its place.
What if they were all to disappear,
    these items that encapsulate me?
Would I be left,
    aimless and confused and undelineated,
grasping at froth
    to clothe my insubstantiality
or freed to drift,
    undeterred, unencumbered, unobstructed,
through the eye of a needle?

ENDURANCE TEST

Time, now, is spent
time after time,
waiting for the wound to heal,
      respite from the suffering
      of suffering
      and accumulated sorrow.

What does it serve
to cling
to the impermanent flesh?
The house crumbles
beyond renovation
or rejuvenation
and the great gift
grows burdensome.

Now, as all seeds ripen
and every bill comes due,
the body pays its debt
to attachment.

And this, perhaps,
is the purpose of enduring,
      to calm the waves of karma
      out of compassion
      for who comes hereafter.

FAMILY, GATHERING

Let us not be afraid
to love each other.
Let us accept each other
with no but's
or should be's or if only's.
Let us not say we know each other
too well
or not well enough.
Let us recognize
that we are not wasting our time
on idle speech and superficialities
but speaking from our hearts,
reaching for the whole
that knows each of its parts.

We are converging,
straining toward the climax
of union.
Love draws us
as the avatars,
established in our centres,
pull us inward
until we implode
and open into emptiness.

And if there is no logical excuse
for us to love each other,
let us love each other
beyond reason
until the intellect
catches up with us
and says
"Of course."

SIDETRACKS

I leap,
like a desert-weary traveler,
into the liquid mirage of love.
I have bloodied my knees
and scraped my hands,
bruised myself
against the parched rocks
and scorched sands
of abracadabra delusion,
        plunged myself often
        into confusion,
           awakening from dreams to where
           what was fluid, flowing,
              evaporates into the arid air.
So often, with so little knowing,
has my nomad heart
been there,
ready to rest,
to merge with this
undifferentiated bliss,
only to find the journey not yet ended,
the destination misperceived,
misapprehended.

And I wander,
wondering
where and how and when,
again.

SIN IN MY SEVENTIETH YEAR

I own up,
in varying degrees,
to the seven deadly sins
    – and countless others, more trivial,
but now,
in my three score and tenth year,
I confess, above all, to pride.

I am not too proud
for hand-me-downs and handouts
and even, on occasion, helpful advice.

I am not proud of my looks
    – that was long ago –
nor of my accomplishments,
save that I have survived.

I have no pride of possessions,
    all are impermanent and mutable,
nor of my intellect which, like my body,
is swiftly succumbing to the indignities of age.

I might take pride in the kind hearts
of my children but,
fearing the jealousy of the gods,
I shall keep silent.

But I am proud,
fiercely and joyously proud,
simply of being here,
of existing at this time and place
in the continuum of consciousness,
as witness and participant.

I am proud that I have been summoned
by the universe
to learn its ways,
to serve the great work as lover and beloved.

I am so proud to be a drop
in the bucket of totality,
a spark in the blazing glory of creation.

I am proud, beyond measure,
    like a freshman at the senior prom,
of having been invited to the dance.

Vernal Equinox

COURT ETIQUETTE

In my golden years, I've come to see
what relationships work for me
and I confess that most men bore me
unless they totally adore me.
So, since I am no longer shy,
I tell each gent that happens by

> If you want to catch my eye,
> you're really going to have to try.
> Reticence, in the slightest measure,
> is not a quality I treasure
> when it comes to compliments.
> Commend my charm, my wit, my sense.
> Say my work is meaningful,
> soulful and insightful.
> Tell me I am utterly,
> in every way, delightful,
> that, upon sincere reflection,
> I exemplify perfection.
> Tell me I've been underrated,
> tell me that you're captivated,
> that you'd risk both life and limb
> to satisfy my slightest whim.
> Swear that I'm the finest yet
> of all the women you have met.
> When it comes to adulation,
> do not be abstemious;
> put me on a pedestal
> and pelt me with gardenias.
> Send me roses and an orchid;
> that is what your fortune's for, kid.
> Give me things that Cartier sells.
> Buy me meals in fine hotels;
> never let me see the bill.
> Say I'm mentioned in your will.

Glorify the present me,
not what I was or who I'll be.
Sing my praises far and wide
as pulchritude personified.

I tell this to the image makers,
the cops, the butchers and the bakers,
the sloths, the movers and the shakers.
                    I don't get a lot of takers.

GERIATRIC VALENTINE

When the pheromones have weakened
and the chemistry is odd,
will we still be held together
though the bonds are frayed and flawed?

With the drying of the juices
and the damping of the lust,
do you think we could be left with
an emotion we can trust?

When estrogen's exhausted
and testosterone has dwindled,
will we still have more in common
than a spark that can't be kindled?

When our passions have been tempered
and our gonads have been tamed,
can we warm each other's cockles
without getting all inflamed?

If our pleasure centres petrify
when dopamine deprived,
will we find our hearts still tender?
Will affection have survived

or will we be separated
by a wide, abysmal chasm
when we concede that there is
no potential for orgasm?

I'd be very disappointed,
I'd be terribly distressed
if we found we have no mutual attraction
when we're dressed.

BETTER LATE

With fancy footwork,
avoiding slips,
we managed never
to come to grips.

Because the facts
were a flimsy tissue,
we mindfully stepped
around the issue.

Not being predisposed
to lie,
we put it off
and put it by.

We softly put it
to one side,
unacknowledged,
but not denied.

Both of us feared
to take the chance,
to walk the walk
and dance the dance.

We whirled and dipped
with measured art,
keeping meticulously
apart.

I was so careful,
so very discreet,
you were so terribly
fast on your feet.

We felt no emotions
we didn't disguise.
You were so wary
and I was so wise.

You were frightened,
I was flattered;
both of us chose to
assume that it mattered.

We came to almost
and perhaps,
then let it go
and let it lapse.

For all your failings
and all my faults,
now hold me close
and let us waltz.

FALLING FLAT

We made some sparks and we made some light,
we made some noises in the night,
we made a merry time all right,
but we never made music.

We made a picture, chic and smart,
of excellence in head and heart.
We made ourselves a work of art,
but we never made music.

We made an effort, more or less,
the best that we could do, I guess.
We made a moderate success,
but we never made music.

We made a modicum of hay,
We made our uncommitted way.
We made some moves that made our day,
but we never made music.

We made no effort to deceive,
we tucked no ace up any sleeve.
We made a game of make believe,
but we never made music.

We made it through from dusk to dawn,
but your memory is almost gone,
for only melody lingers on
and we never did make music.

FOOTNOTE

I never didn't love you,
I just couldn't make you happy
and that was my shortcoming and my sin.
So I left you to discover,
beyond anger and betrayal,
that happiness arises from within.

I didn't never love you,
but I couldn't make you happy;
I wouldn't be responsible,
I couldn't take the blame.
And it might have been a weakness
or perhaps it was a strength,
but I find I'm pretty happy
and I hope you are the same.

MIRRORS

I like to think myself aware,
she said,
      satisfied with herself,
    a trifle smug,
and reached an elegantly lacquered finger out
and squashed a ladybug.

           I watch, he said,
        and I am totally aware
               on each occasion
                and in every place
       of all my interactions.
           And, so that I should not
           miss the point,
           he leaned towards me
           and shouted in my face.

BOTTOM LINE

Don't tell me how much profit you have made
or how intelligently you invest,
or by what maitre d's you're recognized,
or which elite couturiers you're dressed.

Don't demonstrate how loudly you can pray,
how well in sacred scriptures you are versed.
Tell me the secret longings of your heart
and, of your aspirations, which comes first.

Don't tell me what positions you've attained
in bed or boardroom. I don't want the whole
record of how you've serviced mammon. Just
tell me how well you think you've served your soul.

Tell me how many homeless you have housed,
how many hungry children you have fed.
Tell me what elders you have comforted.
Say now, where have your aspirations led.

Have you been often visited by joy?
How does compassion now transform your day?
How do you stir yourself into the world?
Who are you while your ego is away?

What are your proudest memories in life?
Don't say how fast you drove, how much you earned.
Tell me, instead, the friends you've come to know.
Show me what loving kindness you have learned.

ETYMOLOGY –
NOT TO BE CONFUSED WITH ENTOMOLOGY

There are a certain some, I guess,
raised to ignore la politesse,
who, over puddles spread no coats
and waste no time on thank-you notes,
who are not shamed to be inept
nor blush at promises unkept.
They load the dice and cheat at cards
and walk their dogs in neighbors' yards.
Their heads are big, their hearts are hard,
they hold the truth in low regard.
They've learned the art of obfuscation
and out-and-out prevarication.
They plug into the public's sockets
and use the power to line their pockets
and offer, for their vile abuses,
not apologies, but excuses.

I have a strong and unalloyed suspicion
polite does not derive from politician.

EXPLORING AN ALIEN CIVILIZATION

We have discovered
an old tract
which tells
how the people on this planet
shit in their wells.
They shit in their food
and they shit in their air;
they shit on each other,
everywhere.
They had shit for breakfast
and shit for brains.

And we have found
some artifacts,
but not a single soul remains.

NO FREE LUNCH

You won't always get what you pay for
– I think that's a pretty safe bet –
but some way, sometime, somehow,
you'll pay for what you get.

ENEMIES

We're going to sit down here together
and this is how it will be,
I'll discover something in you to love
and you'll find something in me.

We're going to look into each other's eyes
beyond who's wrong or right,
through persona and personality
until we see the light.

We may not get to be valentines;
we don't have to go that far,
but there's nothing sentimental
in acknowledging who we are.

Though you may not approve of what I say
and I might not like what you do,
still, I'm one of the faces worn by God
and another one is you.

And we're all of us here to learn to love,
to awaken and come to see
that the whole of creation is divine,
including you and me.

EPIPHANY

Last week,
as I passed beneath the branches
of a budding maple,
I was struck,
square atop the head,
by a liquid pigeon dropping.
I think it was a pigeon.
By the time I looked up,
remembering, dilatorily,
to close my mouth,
the culprit had vanished
too quickly for a positive identification.

I stood for a moment,
blotting my pate with a kleenex,
and then resumed my walk,
pondering the cosmic import
of the incident.

What are the odds, I wondered,
against this particular concatenation
of happenings,
this synchronicity of step and sphincter?

I am aware
that such an occurrence
is considered fortunate by some.
Is this mere superstition or, in this case,
a significant phenomenon?
Am I a lucky shithead
or simply an avian latrine?
Is this a heavenly fertilization
that will nurture some meaningful growth,
some momentous expansion?
In which case,
is all the shit in my life
a forerunner of wisdom,
a harbinger of insight,
a compost for consciousness?

I have explored, examined, contemplated
and concluded
that this was a spiritual wake-up call,
a celestial reminder
that even the unlikeliest event
serves
to ring the bell of the Dharma.
     DUNG!

MORE OF THE SAME

In this vale of trials and tears,
when one's in doodoo up to one's ears,
this is what one like me most fears,
more shit.

When one's abused and sad and vexed,
there is no need to be perplexed,
one knows what's going to happen next,
more shit.

When one's tired and troubled, bruised and sore
and thinks that one can take no more,
let me remind you what's in store,
more shit.

Shit by the barrel, shit by the heap,
when you're awake and while you sleep
who dreamed that it could get so deep?
More shit.

It happens morning, noon and night.
We all experience this plight,
just when one thinks one sees the light,
more shit.

When one's surrounded by manure,
one's nervous and one's insecure.
Only of this can one be sure,
more shit.

They say it helps one's garden grow;
I pray that this is truly so,
but what's to come I think I know.
More shit.

One more scoop of poop,
a gigapile of guano,
an additional carload of crap,
another increment of excrement,
more shit.

FIGMENT

Not you,
but someone very like you,
lives in that empty place
within my heart.

His looks are similar to yours,
his body is as excellently built,
    I fit as perfectly into his arms.
His lips are just as soft;
he smiles your crooked tooth.

More fantasy than memory,
he has your sometimes tenderness
and anger does not churn in him.
The honey of his disposition
is not embittered with cruel criticism.

His intellect, like yours, is keen;
his brilliant mind
is not contained within a shell of certainty,
but opens constantly to question.

His laughter is as ready as your own,
and does not rise from mockery.
He is not anchorite or socialite,
but content in his own company;
he does not need me to make him happy.

His love is sweet,
as I remember yours,
and with no aftertaste of jealousy.

Your image and similitude,
he comes to me in dreams,
demanding nothing but our mutual delight.

I do not visit him
as often as I might;
the resemblance is so great
I sometimes grow confused and,
    forgetting painful lessons learned,
think that it is you
I long for.

MINDING MY BUSINESS

A poetry book
is not a money maker;
it is an article of faith,
a statement of illogic,
an exploration
below the bottom line.

Poetry books are not produced
by multi-national corporations
or military-industrial complexes
or bureaucrats or committees
or those to whom profit and power
are the goals of existence.

Poetry is not for the dishonest,
the greedy,
the harborers of ill will.
It is the language
which spirit speaks to spirit,
reminding itself of mutuality.

A poem is a possibility.
It is not contained by concepts;
it confounds expectations.
It is the universal solvent
flung at the barriers of separation
to crack the shell of certainty
and melt the membrane
of the mind that is made up.

It says,
we are all part of an awesome truth,
a magnificent adventure.

Only poetry can voice the ineffable,
channel the ephemeral,
capture the delicate
without damaging its wings.

Let us tell each other our stories,
our insights,
our aspirations.
I am so weary
of party lines and propaganda,
of bombast and dogma
and incomprehensible claptrap.
Talk to me in poetry.
It is all I understand.

Summer Solstice

TAKE YOUR MEDICINE

Let go your curding criticism
and your toxic condemnation.
There has been nothing but the to and fro of love
in everything you ever felt or smelt,
in anything you tasted, touched or saw.
Expand your boundaries;
the less that you reject, the quicker you will heal.
Open wide
and say awe.

NON-DETERMINED

What is reality's uttermost border?
What is enfolded in implicate order?
Is there a limitless sea of potential,
randomly manifest or providential?

I have attended, on many occasions,
lectures illumined with lengthy equations,
erudite seminars studded with very
incomprehensible vocabulary,
concepts of which I could never conceive.

How will I ever know what I believe?

FANCY THIS

I go for refuge
to the primal source,
    the womb of all creation.

From the inchoate stuff
of mind,
I spin potential
into manifestation,
    in crimson threadings
    of desire
        and, winding them
        upon the shuttle
        of visualization,
I weave
a tapestry of fantasy
upon the boundless loom
of actualization.

And when the fabric crumbles into dust,
    as all eventually must,
I hail the glorious disintegration.

All comes from love,
remains as love,
returns to love.
I do not cling.
I let it go.

I take it up
and shape it, once again,
to fit my heart's unceasing jubilation.
    The grace waves
    and the particles,
    in endless undulation,
    are what I make of them.

So I will make a fabric
of gratitude and celebration,
feeding my endless appetite for joy
out of my infinite imagination.

EFFORTLESS PRACTICE

Gather your thoughts from yesterday,
all the fond memories
and sad regrets
and then let them go,
for a brief breath of contemplation.
And collect your dreamings
from tomorrow,
each hope
and every expectation.

Bring to your breath
nothing but emptiness.
Abandon striving, obligation,
duty.
Lay your unconstrained mind
upon the moment.
It will open
and show you its beauty.

A JOYFUL NOISE

Let's hear it for joy.

Joy has become, these days,
an oddity,
a suspect and a sadly
scarce commodity.
Let's lend an ear and give a cheer for joy ...
Three cheers and all the tigers we can roar
superenthusiastically, before
we lose our heaven-sent capacity.

Hooray for joy,
with all of the insouciant audacity
that we can muster.
Without it our prosaic days lack lustre
and life's a dilatory filibuster.

Let's speak a word right now for joy.
Not for that uninformed and transitory bliss
accompanying ignorance,
but with full cognizance for this
torrent of coruscating light
that courses and carouses through our bodies
singing scintillation day and night.
And, though we may not hear a sound,
that song is joy.
Once we discover it
we can exude it and exchange it
and pass it all around
and see the way it fills the universe.

So when we feel that things are bad
and just keep getting worse,
and famine, degradation and disaster rule
and isolation is a certitude
and circumstance is categorically cruel,
we only need remember joy
to harmonize us with creation.
Joy is the path,
and is, with peace, compassion, love,
the destination.
It's nothing that we have to be afraid of,
it is the very stuff that we are made of.

So let's sing out for joy.
Let's shout and whistle, cheer and yell
and beat a drum and blow a horn
and ring a bell
and let each other know
we've found an infinite, eternal truth to tell.
And that is joy.

KARUNA

No act of compassion
is ever wasted.
It never fails;
it purifies us all.
Whatever issues from the heart,
however great,
however small,
shapes us to oneness.

Simply being
the fullness of our being
joins us,
joins us to joy
that, being once encountered,
no pain can ever quite destroy
but move us to compassion.

And when compassion moves us
we meet with love
whatever life may send.

It is the means
that justifies the end.

SOLSTICE

Now that the light returns
and the old rituals are celebrated
in countless ceremonies,
I remind myself
that each of us comes
bearing illumination.

We are all here,
together,
to redeem the sins of the fathers
and the collective karma of our species.
We live, every one,
to learn compassion
and we shall die,
        upon the cross of matter,
for love.

GROUND OF BEING

We need not wait
for a mingling of the ashes;
your dust and my dust
are one.
We are fashioned
by the same hand,
of the same clay,
and when our sojourn here is done
we shall return
to undifferentiated union.

But we need not wait for death
to know communion.

There is an all-encompassing totality
conceiving, birthing, nurturing duality
while underlying indivisible reality.

We are one in the singular Mind,
many in manifestation,
not forsaking integration
but learning individuation.

We are one people
before birth, after death;
I drink your sweat
and you inhale my breath
and nothing in us is discrete.
We need each other to complete
the never-ending process
of ourselves,
our ever-evolving story,
the odyssey of consciousness
born in the dust of stars,
joining and journeying to glory.

LAST WORD

And if I never write again,
have I said all I had to say?
Have I repeated, now, sufficient times
that love is the only road,
the only way?
Have I said,
again and again,
what I said at the start,
        that the only path
        is the path with heart?

That is what I found
at the beginning;
love is the foundation
and the underpinning.
Love is the aspiration
and the realization,
the vehicle
and destination,
the inspiration
and the ultimate cessation.

I've said it from the first,
I've said it all before.
I'll say it for the last time,
        just once more,
the only obligation,
the terminal summation,
the final liberation
is love.

Other books by Linda Stitt
>Reflections from a Dusty Mirror
>What Do You Feed a Unicorn?
>Yesterday's Poetry
>It Was True at the Time
>Insights and Outlooks
>Adjust Your Set

With Charlene Jones and Cecilie Kwiat
>Uncritical Mass in Consort

With Charlene Jones
>Bliss Pig and Other Poems

I want to thank all my friends who have encouraged and supported me throughout the preparation on this book. I am especially grateful to:

>Allan Briesmaster, fellow poet and inimitable editor, without whose expertise and nurturing the bud would never have flowered.

>Morley Chalmers, my longtime buddy, whose typesetting and design talent have contributed greatly to my publications, right from the start.

>Paula Stitt, my daughter, my webmaster, my generous and indefatigable computer guru, whose creative skills are made manifest in many areas of this book.

My mother read poetry to me when I was in her womb and I emerged, I am told, in Huntsville, Ontario, crying in iambic pentameter. With the encouragement of my parents, I was composing verses as soon as I could talk.

I was educated in Georgetown and Toronto and lived for many years in Thunder Bay, where I began the process of what Carl Sagan described as "matter coming to consciousness."

The exploration continues even now that I have exceeded my shelf life and surpassed my best before date.

> In view of the fact that my work has been known,
>   on occasion, to rhyme,
> I consider myself an anachronism
>   in my own time.

May all beings be well and happy.